The Third Industrial Revolution

The Third Industrial Revolution

Technology, Productivity, and Income Inequality

Jeremy Greenwood

The AEI Press

Publisher for the American Enterprise Institute
WASHINGTON, D.C.

1997

Available in the United States from the AEI Press, c/o Publisher Resources Inc., 1224 Heil Quaker Blvd., P.O. Box 7001, La Vergne, TN 37086-7001. Distributed outside the United States by arrangement with Eurospan, 3 Henrietta Street, London WC2E 8LU England.

ISBN 0-8447-7093-0

1 3 5 7 9 10 8 6 4 2

The AEI PRESS
Publisher for the American Enterprise Institute
1150 17th Street, N.W., Washington, D.C. 20036

Printed in the United States of America

Contents

Foreword

This study is one of a series commissioned by the American Enterprise Institute on trends in the level and distribution of U.S. wages, income, wealth, consumption, and other measures of material welfare. The issues addressed in the series involve much more than dry statistics: they touch on fundamental aspirations of the American people—material progress, widely shared prosperity, and just reward for individual effort—and affect popular understanding of the successes and shortcomings of the private market economy and of particular government policies. For these reasons, discussions of "economic inequality" in the media and political debate are often partial and partisan as well as superficial. The AEI series is intended to improve the public discussion by bringing new data to light, exploring the strengths and weaknesses of various measures of economic welfare, and highlighting important questions of interpretation, causation, and consequence.

Each study in the series is presented and discussed in draft form at an AEI seminar prior to publication by the AEI Press. Marvin Kosters, director of economic policy studies at AEI, organized the series and moderated the seminars. A current list of published studies appears on the last page.

CHRISTOPHER DEMUTH
President, American Enterprise Institute

The Third Industrial Revolution

D
id 1974 mark the beginning of a third industrial revolution? Was this the start of an era of rapid technological progress associated with the development of
information technologies (IT)? Did an increase in the pace
of technological advance lead to a rise in income inequality? Is a productivity slowdown related to these phe-
nomena?

The thesis here connects the rate of technological
progress to the level of income inequality and productivity growth. Imagine that a leap in the state of technology
occurs and that this jump is embodied in new machines,
such as information technologies. Suppose that the adoption of new technologies involves a significant cost in
terms of learning and that skilled labor has an advantage
at learning. Then the advance in technology will be associated with an increase in the demand for skill needed to
implement it. Hence, the wages of skilled labor relative
to unskilled labor, or the skill premium, will rise, and income inequality will widen. In the early phases, the new
technologies may not be operated efficiently because of
inexperience. The initial incarnations of ideas into equip-

Thanks go to Marvin Kosters for his helpful comments. This monograph is based on a joint paper with Mehmet Yorukoglu entitled
"1974"; he played a vital role in pursuing this line of research.

1

ment may be far from ideal. Productivity growth may appear to stall as the economy undertakes the (unmeasured) investment in knowledge needed so that the new technologies can approach their full potential. The coincidence of rapid technological change, widening inequality, and slowing productivity growth is not without precedence in economic history.

The Information Age

Figure 1 illustrates the decline in the price of equipment over the postwar period. The figure shows the price of a piece of new producer equipment relative to the price of a unit of nondurable consumer goods and services. Clearly, over the postwar period, producer equipment has become less expensive relative to consumer nondurables and services. This result reflects the fact that the rate of technological change in the producer durable sector has exceeded the consumer nondurable sector. Specifically, due to technological progress, ever-increasing quantities of investment goods can be produced over time, using a given amount of labor and capital; this situation drives their price down. This type of technological advance is dubbed *investment-specific* technological progress since it affects the investment goods sector of the economy.

The price of equipment fell faster after 1974 than before it, as the slopes of the trend lines shows. If the decline in the price of new equipment can be taken as a measure of improved efficiency in equipment production, then the pace of technological change jumped up around 1974. Some economists estimate that 60 percent of postwar U.S. growth may derive from the introduction of new, more efficient equipment.[1] The rapid advance in technology since 1974 is undoubtedly linked to the development of information technologies. The price of computers has plummeted over the postwar period, as figure 2 illustrates. On average, the price of a new computer has

FIGURE 1
PRICE OF NEW PRODUCER EQUIPMENT, RELATIVE TO PRICE OF CONSUMER NONDURABLES AND SERVICES, 1954–1990

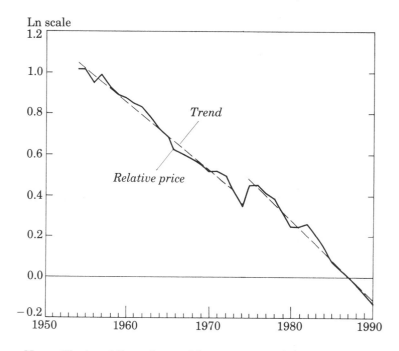

NOTE: The trend lines show a 3.3 percent annual decrease, 1950–1973, and a 4.0 percent annual decrease, after 1974. Ln stands for natural logarithm.
SOURCE: Greenwood, Hercowitz, and Krusell (1996).

dropped around 19 percent a year. Hence, a new computer costing $5,000 in 1987 would have been priced at $2 million in 1955. Figure 3 shows the phenomenal rise of IT investment (as a fraction of total equipment investment). In 1954, information technologies accounted for less than 7 percent of total investment, while they now make up about 50 percent.

Growth in labor productivity stalled with the rise in IT investment, as figure 3 also shows. Labor productivity

FIGURE 2
PRICE OF NEW COMPUTERS, 1955–1987

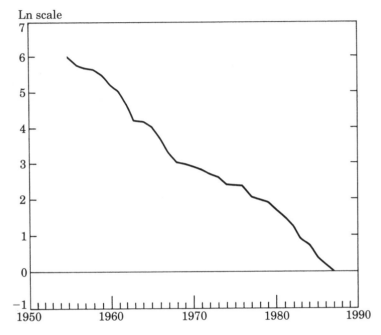

NOTE: Annual average decrease in price is 18.7 percent. Ln stands for natural logarithm.
SOURCE: Yorukoglu (1996).

measures the amount of gross domestic product produced per man-hour worked in the economy. It is often taken as a measure of how efficient labor is in the economy. The more GDP each worker can produce, the better off is the economy. Before 1974, labor productivity grew at about 2 percent per year; after, a paltry 0.8 percent. This change is often referred to as the productivity slowdown. Isn't it somewhat paradoxical that at a time of massive techno-logical advance, due to the introduction of information technologies and the like, the advance in a worker's pro-duce should stall?

FIGURE 3
INVESTMENT IN INFORMATION TECHNOLOGY AND LABOR PRODUCTIVITY, 1948–1994

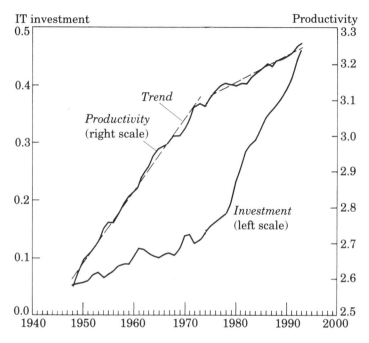

NOTE: IT investment is the ratio of such investment to total equipment investment. Productivity is measured on a natural logarithmic scale. The trend line before 1974 shows a 2 percent annual growth rate; after 1974, 0.8 percent.
SOURCE: National Income and Product Accounts and Citibase.

By most accounts, wage inequality increased around 1974. Some postwar measures of income inequality are shown in figure 4.[2] The percentage gap between the average wage earned by the upper quartile (seventy-fifth percentile) and the average wage earned by the lower quartile (twenty-fifth percentile) remained roughly constant between 1959 and 1970. From 1970 to 1988, this gap increased by twenty-two percentage points. That is,

FIGURE 4
WAGE INEQUALITY: WAGE GAPS AT DIFFERENT POINTS IN THE DISTRIBUTION, 1959–1988

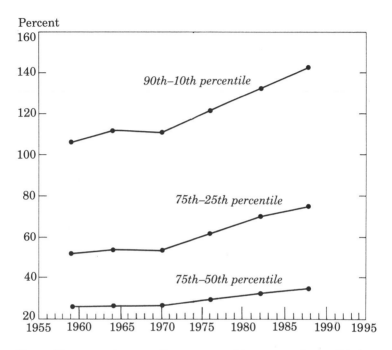

NOTE: The percentage gap for wages used to measure inequality is the difference in the natural logarithms of wages at different points in the distribution.
SOURCE: Juhn, Murphy, and Pierce (1993).

in 1970, there was a 53 percent gap in wage income between the two groups; in 1988, it was 75 percent. The other measures behave similarly.

The Industrial Revolution

The Industrial Revolution, begun in 1760, symbolizes investment-specific technological change. This period witnessed the birth of several technological miracles.[3]

Crompton's mule revolutionized the spinning of cotton. Next, Watt's energy-efficient steam engine brought steam power to manufacturing. The main cost of a steam engine was operating it: it was a hungry beast. A Watt steam engine cost £500–800 (McPherson 1994, 16). Operating a steam engine, though, was enormously expensive. Each consumed £3,000 of coal per annum.[4] By comparison, 500 horses, which apparently could produce the same amount of work, cost only £900 in feed. Thus, the pursuit of an energy-efficient steam engine was on. The older Newcomen steam engine of 1769 needed 30 pounds of coal per horsepower hour, while a Watt engine of 1776 required 7.5 pounds. By 1850 or so, this number had been reduced to 2.5. So the cost of steam power fell dramatically over the course of the Industrial Revolution. When the spinning mule was harnessed to steam power, the mechanization of manufacturing was inexorable. By 1841, the real price of spun cotton had fallen by two-thirds. In 1784, Cort introduced his puddling and rolling technique for making wrought iron, a product vital for the industrialization of Britain. Between 1788 and 1815, the production of wrought iron increased by 500 percent. The price of wrought iron fell from £22 to £14 per ton from 1801 to 1815, despite the fact that between 1770 and 1815 the general level of prices rose by 50 percent. Last, the foundation of the modern machine-tool industry was constructed. A gun-barreling machine designed by Wilkinson could make cylinders for Watt's steam engines. Maudley introduced the heavy-duty lathe.

Skill undoubtedly played an important role in technological innovation and adoption during the Industrial Revolution. While it was the age of a handful of miracles, many historians also view it as an age of continuous and gradual smaller innovations and an age of learning. Implementing and operating brilliant inventions and effecting subsequent innovations is often demanding work requiring skill. It took three months, for instance, for someone brought up in a mill to learn how to operate either a hand mule or a self-acting mule (von Tunzelmann 1994). The former required three years to learn to maintain, while the latter demanded seven. Knowledge concerning improvements in the machinery continued throughout the worker's lifetime. It seems reasonable to conjecture that the demand for skill rose in the Industrial Revolution as "for the economy *as a whole* to switch from manual techniques to a mechanized production required hundreds of inventors, thousands of innovating entrepreneurs and tens of thousands of mechanics, technicians and dexterous rank and file workers."[5] In fact, income inequality rose throughout the Industrial Revolution, as plotted in figure 5.[6]

The diffusion of new technologies is often slow because the initial fabrications of the underlying ideas are inefficient. Getting new technologies to operate at their full potential may take considerable time. Thus, a new technology's productivity may be low at first. Cort's famous puddling and rolling process went through a long incubation period and was commercially unsuccessful at first (von Tunzelmann 1994). Royalties had to be slashed to encourage adoption. Apparently, "both entrepreneurs and workers had to go through a learning period, making many mistakes that often resulted in low outputs of uneven quality."[7] Growth in productivity fell in the initial stages of the Industrial Revolution, as shown in figure 5.[8] Before the Industrial Revolution, productivity was growing at 0.4 percent a year. With the coming of the new era, productivity growth fell to an annual rate of 0.2 percent. This decline lasted for forty years. Was this slump in productivity growth connected to the teething pains of adopting new technologies? As the revolution spread, productivity growth picked up. Seventy years into the revolution, it was growing at a much more robust 0.5 percent. Thus, the fruits of the Industrial Revolution took time to ripen.

FIGURE 5
PRODUCTIVITY AND INEQUALITY IN BRITAIN DURING THE INDUSTRIAL REVOLUTION

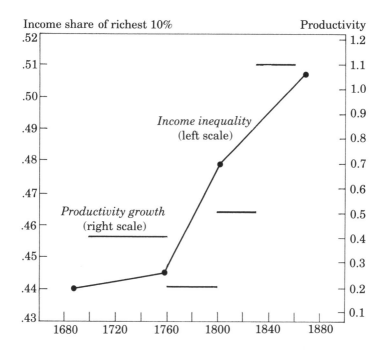

NOTE: Productivity is the average growth rate of labor productivity in the given period.
SOURCE: Harley (1993) and Lindert and Williamson (1983).

The American Antebellum Period

The Industrial Revolution spread to the United States around 1840. This was an era of tremendous investment-specific technological change. The nation industrialized at a rapid clip. Figure 6 shows the dramatic decline in the price of new equipment (relative to all goods).[9] Presumably, this decrease reflects improved efficiency in the production of new equipment: more equipment could be

FIGURE 6
U.S. EQUIPMENT PRICES, PRODUCTIVITY, AND INEQUALITY, 1800–1870

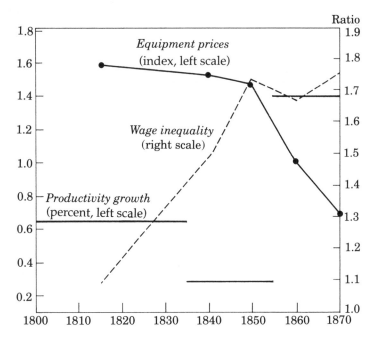

NOTE: Equipment prices are prices of new equipment relative to all goods. Productivity is measured on a natural logarithmic scale. Wage inequality is a measure of the skill premium.
SOURCE: Abramovitz and David (1973, table 2); Gallman (1992); and Williamson and Lindert (1980, appendix D).

produced for less. One would expect that this decline in the price of new equipment should have encouraged more investment. For the period 1774–1815, the real stock of equipment per capita grew at roughly 0.7 percent per year. Between 1815 and 1860, however, the average annual growth was a robust 2.8 percent. This jumped to a whopping 4.5 percent from 1860 to 1900. Two examples illustrate this incredible pace of industrialization. In

1830, there were just 30 miles of railroad tracks in the United States. By 1840, this had risen to 2,808 miles, while, in 1860, the number was 30,000.[10] Likewise, the aggregate capacity of U.S. steam engines more than quadrupled from 1840 to 1860, from 760,000 to 3,470,000 horsepower. That capacity rose another one and a half times by 1870, to 5,590,000. The antebellum period saw a dramatic surge in the skill premium, as figure 6 illustrates. Not surprisingly, skilled workers, such as engineers, machinists, boilermakers, carpenters, and joiners, all saw their wages rise relative to the common laborer. Last, there was a slowdown in labor productivity growth for the 1840s, just as the American Industrial Revolution was gaining steam; the annual growth rates of labor productivity are plotted in figure 6.

The Hypothesis

The adoption of new technologies involves a significant cost in terms of learning; skill facilitates this learning process. That is, skill is important for adapting to change. There is considerable evidence for learning effects. Using a data set from 1973 to 1986 consisting of 2,000 firms from forty-one industries, for example, Bahk and Gort (1993) find that a plant's productivity increases by 15 percent over the first fourteen years of its life because of learning effects.

There is also evidence that skill plays an important role in facilitating the adoption of new technologies. Farmers with high levels of education adopt agricultural innovations earlier than farmers with low levels. Findings reported in Bartel and Lichtenberg (1987) support the joint hypothesis that (1) educated workers have a comparative advantage in implementing new technologies because they are better at assimilating new ideas and (2) the demand for educated relative to less-educated workers declines as experience is gained with a technology. Apparently, for each year equipment ages, skilled labor's share of the wage bill drops 0.78 percentage points. This relationship suggests that less-skilled labor is needed as production experience with equipment is gained through time. Using a cross-country data set, Flug and Hercowitz (1996) find that a rise in equipment investment leads to an increase in the skill premium and to higher relative employment for skilled labor. In particular, a 1 percentage point increase in the equipment investment–to–output ratio leads to a 1.90 percentage point increase in the skilled-to-unskilled employment ratio. High investment in equipment seems to imply a high demand for skilled labor, which is used to ease the process of adoption.

The hypothesis developed here is different from the capital-skill complementarity hypothesis.[11] The latter states that skilled labor is more complementary with capital in production than is unskilled labor—or, more or less equivalently, that capital substitutes better for unskilled labor than skilled labor. The recent rise in the skill premium is consistent with capital-skill complementarity and an increase in the rate of investment-specific technological change.[12] The idea in this monograph, however, is that a successful adoption of a new technology requires skilled labor. Moreover, as a technology becomes established, the production process substitutes away from expensive skilled labor toward more economical unskilled labor. Therefore, in times of heightened technological progress, the demand for skill should rise since this type of labor has a comparative advantage in speeding up and easing the process of technological adoption. Such times should therefore be associated with a rise in the skill premium. If this notion is correct, once the recent burst of investment-specific technological change subsides, as IT matures, the skill premium should decline.[13]

How large are the costs of technological adoption? Calculations suggest that the costs of adopting new technologies exceed inventions cost by a factor of twenty to one, and that adoption costs may amount to 10 percent of GDP (Jovanovic 1996). Surely, the costs of technological adoption must be large. How else can the long diffusion lags for new technologies be explained, as well as the continual investment in old dominated technologies at the level of households, firms, and countries? And, surely, a large part of these adoption costs must be in acquiring or developing the skills needed to implement the new technologies.

The Learning Curve

As a case in point for the importance of learning effects, consider the Lawrence Number 2 mill, a cotton mill in the antebellum period studied by David (1975). This facility was built in 1834 in Lowell, Massachusetts. Detailed inventories of the equipment at this plant show that no new machinery was added between 1836 and 1856. Thus, it seems reasonable to infer that any increases in productivity over this period arose purely because of learning effects. In fact, output per manhour in this plant grew on average at 2.3 percent per year over this period. Figure 7 shows the plant's learning curve. The four observations pertain to years when the plant was known to be operating at full capacity.

Learning curves from angioplasty surgery, flight control simulation, munitions manufacturing, and steel finishing are documented in Jovanovic and Nyarko (1995); there are a plethora of other examples in the literature. Yorukoglu (1996) has studied the learning curve for information technologies, using data from 297 firms over the period 1987–1991. His learning curve for information technologies, showing strong learning effects, is plotted in figure 8. The service flow (similar to horsepower for a steam engine) captured from new computers increases dramatically over time. This flow grows at ap-

FIGURE 7
PRODUCTIVITY AT THE LAWRENCE NUMBER 2 COTTON
MILL, 1839–1856

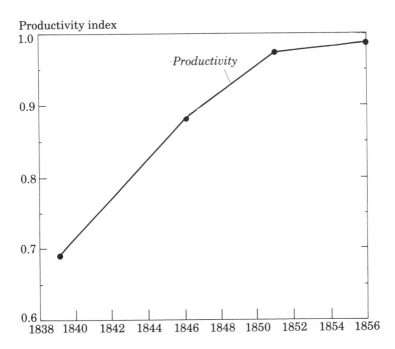

SOURCE: David (1975).

proximately 28 percent (compounded) per year. Two words of caution are offered here. First, as the error bands show, the range of estimates is quite high: the data set permitted studying only a small number of firms for a short period.[14] Second, a firm uses more than computers to produce output. If computers account for 5 percent of output, this translates into an output growth rate due to learning alone of about 1.4 percent (.28 × .05 × 100 percent) a year.

Often, learning about a technology comes through use by the final purchaser. Important operating charac-

FIGURE 8
PRODUCTIVITY AND INFORMATION TECHNOLOGY, 1987–1991

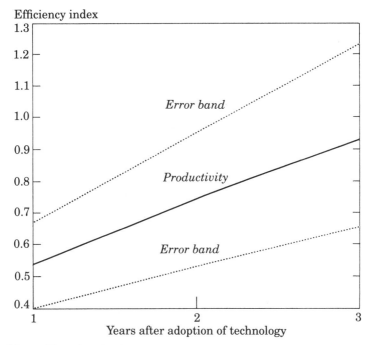

Efficiency index

Error band

Productivity

Error band

Years after adoption of technology

NOTE: Error bands show estimates of 95 percent confidence intervals.
SOURCE: Yorukoglu (1996).

teristics about some products—such as software—are revealed only after intensive use. Manufacturers may then adjust the product on the basis of feedback from purchasers. The process may take many iterations. The aircraft industry provides an excellent example of such learning by using (Rosenberg 1982). As confidence about the operating characteristics of the DC-8 airplane grew through experience, the manufacturer increased the thrust of the engines, while reducing fuel consumption, and modified the wings to lower drag. These modifications eventually allowed the airplane to be stretched from its capacity of 123 to 251 seats. A dramatic improvement in operating costs—such as a 50 percent savings in the fuel costs per seat mile—resulted. For complicated products, reliability is a major concern. Here, maintenance experience proves invaluable. For aircraft, maintenance may account for 30 percent of the operating costs associated with labor and materials. This figure excludes the lost revenue associated with downtime. The costs of servicing new types of jet engines fall dramatically after their introduction. After a decade of operation, maintenance costs have typically dropped to 30 percent of their initial level.

The Diffusion Curve

The adoption of new technologies is notoriously slow. The initial materialization of new ideas is often expensive and plagued with bugs. The impact that investment-specific technological change has on income and productivity is likely to be tempered by two interrelated factors: the speed of learning and the speed of diffusion. The more costly it is for economic agents to learn about a new technology, the slower will be its speed of diffusion. But the faster a new technology diffuses through an economy, the easier it may be to learn about it. Thus, there is a feedback loop between the cost of adoption and the extent of adoption. If a new technology represents a radical or discrete departure from past technologies, society's knowledge about it may be quite limited at first. As the use of the technology becomes widespread, society's stock of experience with it increases, and the technology's productivity rises.

New technologies have high prices when they are first produced. Prices drop as the manufacturer gains experience in production. This encourages adoption, which, in turn, fuels further price declines as production costs fall because of learning and scale effects. Waves of imitators enter the industry, leading to more competitive pricing. The odds of imitating a new invention depend on the number of firms who have already successfully produced the new invention. The number of firms increases through time, making imitation easier. Firms also rush in to produce complementary products, such as software or communication devices for computers. The original product may then have to be modified to incorporate new and better products. To bring these complementary products on line may take a lot of time and resources. The availability of such products encourages further adoption, and so on. An invention may take a long time to bear fruit.

There is considerable evidence that the diffusion of new innovations is slow. In a classic study, Gort and Klepper (1982) examined 46 product innovations, beginning with phonograph records in 1887 and ending with lasers in 1960. The authors traced diffusion by examining the number of firms producing the new product over time. On average, only two or three firms were producing each new product for the first fourteen years after its commercial development; then the number of firms sharply increased (on average six firms per year over the next ten years). Prices fell rapidly following the inception of a product (13 percent a year for the first twenty-four years). Using a twenty-one-product subset of the Gort and Klepper data, Jovanovic and Lach (1996) report that the output of a new product took approximately fifteen years to rise from the 10 percent to the 90 percent diffusion level. They also cite evidence from a study of 265 innovations that a new innovation took forty-one years, on average, to move from the 10 percent to the 90 percent diffusion level. Finally, in the United States, the steam locomotive moved from the 10 percent to the 90 percent diffusion level in fifty-four years, and the diesel (a smaller innovation), twelve years. The diffusion curve for diesels is plot-

FIGURE 9
DIFFUSION CURVE: PREVALENCE OF DIESEL LOCOMOTIVES IN THE UNITED STATES, 1925–1970

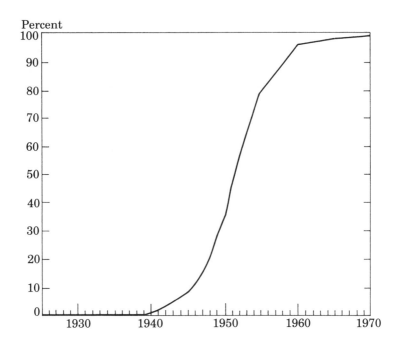

NOTE: Diesels as percentage of total locomotives in use.
SOURCE: *Historical Statistics of the United States,* 1790–1970.

ted in figure 9: after the diesel locomotive was introduced in 1925, diesels took twenty-five years to account for half the locomotives in use.

The Computer and the Dynamo

The metamorphosis of a novel idea into a productive technology, as mentioned, can take a long time.[15] The course of a technology's development is uncharted at its infancy. Electricity and computers are two interesting examples of this uncertain process. Ironically, one of the least productive inventions of the Industrial Revolution is the foundation of the current Information Age. Sometime between 1823 and 1832, Charles Babbage created his difference engine, a mechanical computer. Part of the insight for this invention came from a binary-coded loom invented in 1801 by Jean-Marie Jacquard that used punchcards to control fabric patterns. But, less than fifty years ago, the coming of an information age still was *not* obvious. Just after World War II, *Popular Mechanics* (March 1949) wrote, "Where a calculator on the ENIAC is equipped with 18,000 vacuum tubes and weighs 30 tons, computers in the future may only have 1,000 vacuum tubes and weigh only 1½ tons."

The Electrification of America. The electrification of America, as masterfully chronicled and analyzed by David (1991), illustrates the delays in the successful exploitation of new technologies. The era of electricity dawned around 1900, in the midst of the Second Industrial Revolution. The Second Industrial Revolution, typically dated as starting in the 1860s and ending in the 1930s, saw the birth of the modern chemical industry and the internal combustion engine, in addition to electricity. Electricity was obviously useful as a source of lighting in homes and businesses, but it had to supplant water and steam as the source of power in manufacturing.[16] This process was complicated by the large stocks of equipment and structures already in place and geared to these sources of power. Thus, in the early stages, electricity tended to be overlaid onto existing systems. In particular, the mechanics of steam and water power favored one power unit driving a group of machines. Hence, early electric motors were also used to drive a group of machines. The benefits of electricity derived from the savings in power requirements and the greater control over machine speed. The group-drive system of belts and shafting used by steam and water power was retained. Not surprisingly, electric power tended to be used mostly in rapidly expanding industries since new plants could be designed to accommodate this power source better. By around 1910, it was apparent that machines could be driven with individual electric motors. This consideration had a large impact on productivity in the workplace. The belt-drive apparatus used in the group-drive system could be abandoned. Factory construction no longer needed to allow for the heavy shafting and belt-housing required for the group-drive power transmission. Additionally, the labor needed to maintain this system was eliminated. Furthermore, flexibility in the production process rose for several reasons. The entire power system no longer needed to be shut down for maintenance or replacement purposes. Also, since each machine could be more accurately controlled, increases in the quantity and quality of output obtained. Machines could now be located and moved more freely to accommodate better the production process. Last, the workplace was made considerably safer. Figure 10 shows the diffusion of electric motors in manufacturing. Electric motor horsepower, as a fraction of the horsepower of the total mechanical drive in manufacturing establishments, follows a typical S-shaped diffusion pattern. Labor productivity growth in manufacturing slowed down at the time of electricity's introduction.

In 1890, an astute observer might have understood the importance of electricity for lighting homes and powering factories. He would not have predicted how it would transform lives through the other inventions it would spawn: radio, television, and computers.

The Computerization of America. As with the electrification of America, reaping the harvest from the information technology revolution has not been immediate. The era of computers saw daybreak in the 1950s (Jon-

FIGURE 10
LABOR PRODUCTIVITY AND THE EXTENT OF
ELECTRIFICATION IN U.S. MANUFACTURING, 1889–1948

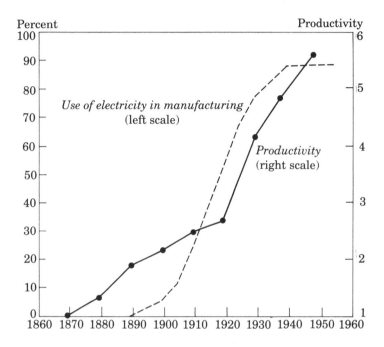

NOTE: Electrification refers to electric motor horsepower as a percentage of manufacturing horsepower. Productivity is measured on a natural logarithmic scale.
SOURCE: David (1991, tables 2 and 3).

scher 1994). Early computers were essentially calculating devices used primarily in academic and industrial research; they performed calculations that were impractical or impossible to do manually. The cost of number crunching declined rapidly over this period. Between 1950 and 1980, the cost of a MIPs (million instructions per second) fell by 27–50 percent per year. This economy spurred the use of computers as calculating devices. The adoption of computers led, in turn, to further price reductions, as computer manufacturers rode up their learning curves, a feedback loop. The 1960s saw computers become file-keeping devices used by businesses to store, sort and process, and retrieve large volumes of data. They saved on labor involved in information-processing activities. The cost of storage probably fell at an annual rate of 25–30 percent from 1960 to 1985. More recently, computers have evolved into communication devices, beginning in the 1970s with the advent of remote accessing and networking. This evolution allowed a partial liberation of the computer from the "clean room." The umbilical cord to the clean room was finally cut in the 1980s with the introduction of the personal computer and the spread of networking.

IT is likely to lead to much more streamlined corporate structures by economizing on the number of employees involved in activities associated with information collection and processing. The goal of any firm is simple: maximize profits. To do this, the firm must have an organizational structure capable of detecting profit opportunities, directing actions to harvest them, and monitoring and evaluating the returns on its activities. These activities largely involve handling and processing information. By 1980, there were 1.13 times as many information workers as production workers, as opposed to just 0.22 in 1900. IT can do much of this information collection and processing activity more efficiently than labor, eliminating the need for battalions of clerks, pools of secretaries, scores of purchasing agents, and layers of supervisors and administrators. Headquarters, design centers, plants, and purchasing and sales offices can now be directly linked to one another by information technologies. The effects of such major changes in business structure may take some time to transpire, but they will inevitably lead to an increase in labor productivity as more output can be produced with less labor. Studies, such as Brynjolfsson and Hitt (1993), indicate that this is now happening. How realistic is the hypothesis presented above? To judge this, Greenwood and Yorukoglu (1996) developed an economic model of the Information Age, which is simulated on a computer. The model incorporates two assumptions: (1) firms face a learning curve when they adopt a new technology and (2) firms can travel up this learning curve faster by hiring skilled labor. With the dawning of the Information Age, the growth rate in labor productivity slumps in the model economy, and income inequality widens. It takes time for the effects of the Information Age to work their way through the system. In the model, productivity growth does not surpass its old level for about twenty years, and the level of productivity does not cross its old trend line—the path that productivity would have traveled along if it had continued at its old growth rate—for forty years. Unskilled wages fall during initial stages of the Information Age. Twenty years elapse before this loss in unskilled wages is made up, and about fifty go by before wages cross their old trend path. Interestingly, during the early stages of the Information Age, the stock market booms as it capitalizes the higher rates of return offered by the new investment opportunities. For many in the economy, though, waiting for the benefits of technological miracles will be like watching grass grow—but it will grow.

Conclusion

Plunging prices for new technologies, a surge in wage inequality, and a slump in the advance of labor productivity—could this be the hallmark of the dawn of another industrial revolution? Just as the steam engine shook eighteenth-century England and electricity rattled nineteenth-century America, are information technologies now rocking the twentieth-century economy?

The story told here is simple. Technological innovation is embodied in the form of new producer durables or services. The prices of these goods decline rapidly in periods of high innovation. Adopting new technologies is costly. Setting up and operating new technologies often involve acquiring and processing new information. Skill facilitates this adoption process. Therefore, times of rapid technological advancement should be associated with a rise in the return to skill. At the dawn of an industrial revolution, the long-run advance in labor productivity temporarily pauses as economic agents undertake the (unmeasured) investment in information required to get new technologies operating closer to their full potential.

How will this affect people's lives? In the long run, everybody will gain. Technological change implies that more output can eventually be produced by a unit of labor. Hence, a unit of labor becomes more valuable. Given time, this factor translates into higher wages and standards of living for everyone. Clearly, everybody today is better off because of the British Industrial Revolution. This was not true, however, in 1760. What about the short run? Skilled workers will fare better than unskilled ones. This disparity will shrink over time for two reasons. First, as information technologies mature, the level of skill needed to work them will decline. Firms will substitute away from expensive skilled labor toward more economical unskilled labor. As this happens, the skill premium will decline. Second, young workers will tend to migrate away from low-paying unskilled jobs toward high-paying skilled ones. This tendency will increase the supply of skilled agents and reduce the amount of unskilled labor, easing the pressure on the skill premium. Additionally, in the short run, the wealthy will do better than the poor. The introduction of new technologies leads to exciting profit opportunities for those with the wherewithal to invest in them. These profit opportunities will shrink over time as the pool of unexploited ideas dries up.

On average, the old have more capital to invest than the young. Thus, in the short run, young, unskilled agents fare the worst. But in the long run, the rising tide of technological change will lift everybody's boat.

Notes

1. Greenwood, Hercowitz, and Krusell (1996) break down U.S. postwar growth into its sources in terms of investment-specific and other forms of technological change.
2. The data are from Juhn, Murphy, and Pierce (1993, table 1.B).
3. This is chronicled in Mokyr (1994).
4. The source is the classic book by Landes (1969, 99–103). Landes (99–101) quotes a writer in 1778: "The vast consumption of fuel in these engines is an immense drawback on the profits of our mines, for every fire-engine of magnitude consumes £3,000 of coals per annum. This heavy tax amounts almost to a prohibition."
5. Mokyr (1994, 29). Interestingly, Mokyr emphatically states that the notion that Britain's Industrial Revolution developed from its more advanced science is false. Rather, ideas flowed from the Continent to Britain, and then working technologies flowed back from Britain to the Continent. Mokyr cites (38) an engineer of the day as stating "the prevailing talent of English and Scottish people was to apply new ideas to use and to bring such applications to perfection, but they do not imagine as much as foreigners." Mokyr (39) concludes that "Britain's technological strength during the industrial revolution depended above all on the abundance and quality of its skilled mechanics and practical technicians who could turn great insights into productive applications."
6. This is documented in Lindert and Williamson (1983, table 3).
7. The quote is by C. K. Hyde (1977), *Technological Change and the British Iron Industry,* as cited by von Tunzelmann (1994, 277).
8. As calculated by Harley (1993, table 3.5).
9. This series is based on calculations using data presented in Gallman (1992).
10. In 1840, roughly 30 percent of pig iron production was devoted to producing railway tracks, and the railway was using 30

percent of the country's steampower capacity (McPherson 1994, chap. 3).

11. The hypothesis was originally advanced by Griliches (1969). A modern reincarnation can be found in Krusell et al. (1996).

12. Krusell et al. (1996) make this case.

13. By contrast, this is not an implication of the capital-skill complementarity hypothesis. Suppose that skilled labor is more complementary with equipment than is unskilled labor. Then, other things equal, the skill premium should rise so long as the stock of equipment increases. That is, there should be a *secular or long-run* rise in the skill premium. See ibid. for more detail.

14. The error bands show the 95 percent confidence intervals.

15. The section title is borrowed from David (1991).

16. While only 3 percent of households used electric lighting in 1899, almost 70 percent did by 1929 (David 1991, table 3).

References

Abramovitz, M., and P. A. David. 1973. "Reinterpreting Economic Growth: Parables and Realities." *American Economic Review* 63: 428–39.

Bahk, B. H., and M. Gort. 1993. "Decomposing Learning by Doing in Plants." *Journal of Political Economy* 101: 561–83.

Bartel, A. P., and F. R. Lichtenberg. 1987. "The Comparative Advantage of Educated Workers in Implementing New Technologies." *Review of Economics and Statistics* 69: 1–11.

Brynjolfsson, B., and L. Hitt. 1993. "Computers and Growth." Unpublished paper. Sloan School of Management, MIT.

David, P. A. 1975. "The 'Horndal Effect' in Lowell, 1834–56: A Short-Run Learning Curve for Integrated Cotton Textile Mills." In *Technical Choice, Innovation and Economic Growth: Essays on American and British Economic Experience*. London: Cambridge University Press.

————. 1991. "Computer and Dynamo: The Modern Productivity Paradox in a Not-Too-Distant Mirror." In *Technology and Productivity: The Challenge for Economic Policy*. Paris: Organization for Economic Cooperation and Development.

Flug, K., and Z. Hercowitz. 1996. "Some International Evidence on Equipment-Skill Complementarity." Unpublished paper. Department of Economics, Tel Aviv University.

Gallman, R. E. 1992. "American Economic Growth before the Civil War." In *American Growth and Standard of Living before the Civil War,* edited by R. E. Gallman and J. J. Wallis. Chicago: University of Chicago Press.

Gort, M., and S. Klepper. 1982. "Time Paths in the Diffusions of Product Innovations." *Economic Journal* 92: 630–53.

Greenwood, J., Z. Hercowitz, and P. Krusell. 1996. "Long-Run Implications of Investment-Specific Technological Change." *American Economic Review.*

Greenwood, J., and M. Yorukoglu. 1996. "1974." Working Paper 429. Rochester Center for Economic Research, W. Allen Wallis Institute for Political Economy, University of Rochester.

Griliches, Z. 1969. "Capital-Skill Complementarity." *Review of Economics and Statistics* 45: 465–68.

Harley, C. K. 1993. "Reassessing the Industrial Revolution: A Macro View." In *The British Industrial Revolution: An Economic Perspective,* edited by J. Mokyr. Boulder: Westview Press.

Jonscher, C. 1994. "An Economic Study of the Information Technology Revolution. In *Information Technology and the Corporation of the 1990s,* edited by T. J. Allen and M. S. Scott Morton. Oxford: Oxford University Press.

Jovanovic, B. 1996. "Learning and Growth." In *Advances in Economics,* edited by D. Kreps and K. F. Wallis. New York: Cambridge University Press.

Jovanovic, B., and S. Lach. 1996. "Product Innovation and the Business Cycle." *International Economic Review,* forthcoming.

Jovanovic, B., and Y. Nyarko. 1995. "A Bayesian Learning Model Fitted to a Variety of Empirical Learning Curves." *Brookings Papers on Economic Activity, Microeconomics:* 247–99.

Juhn, C., K. M. Murphy, and B. Pierce. 1993. "Wage Inequality and the Rise in the Returns to Skill." *Journal of Political Economy* 101: 410–42.

Krusell, P., L. Ohanian, J.-V. Rios-Rull, and L. V. Giovanni.

1996. "Capital-Skill Complementarity and Inequality." Unpublished paper. Department of Economics, University of Rochester.

Landes, D. S. 1969. *The Unbound Prometheus: Technological Change and Industrial Development in Western Europe from 1750 to the Present.* London: Cambridge University Press.

Lindert, P. H., and J. G. Williamson. 1983. "Reinterpreting Britain's Social Tables, 1688–1913." *Explorations in Economic History* 20: 94–109.

McPherson, N. 1994. *Machines and Growth: The Implications for Growth Theory of the History of the Industrial Revolution.* Westport, Conn.: Greenwood Press.

Mokyr, J. 1994. "Technological Change, 1700–1830." In *The Economic History of Britain since 1700,* edited by R. Floud and D. McCloskey. New York: Cambridge University Press.

Rosenberg, N. 1982. "Learning by Using." In *Inside the Black Box: Technology and Economics.* London: Cambridge University Press.

von Tunzelmann, N. 1994. "Technology in the Early Nineteenth Century." In *The Economic History of Britain since 1700,* edited by R. Floud and D. McCloskey. New York: Cambridge University Press.

Williamson, J. G., and P. H. Lindert. 1980. *American Inequality: A Macroeconomic History.* New York: Academic Press.

Yorukoglu, M. 1996. "The Information Technology Productivity Paradox." Unpublished paper. Department of Economics, University of Chicago.

About the Author

JEREMY GREENWOOD is professor of economics at the University of Rochester. He previously held a position at the University of Western Ontario and has been a visiting scholar at the Federal Reserve Bank of Minneapolis and the Institute for International Economic Studies. Mr. Greenwood has written numerous articles on business cycles and growth for academic journals. The work in this monograph has been featured in *Investor's Business Daily, Newsweek,* and the *Nightly Business Report.*

The American Enterprise Institute for Public Policy Research

Founded in 1943, AEI is a nonpartisan, nonprofit, research and educational organization based in Washington, D.C. The Institute sponsors research, conducts seminars and conferences, and publishes books and periodicals.

AEI's research is carried out under three major programs: Economic Policy Studies; Foreign Policy and Defense Studies; and Social and Political Studies. The resident scholars and fellows listed in these pages are part of a network that also includes ninety adjunct scholars at leading universities throughout the United States and in several foreign countries.

The views expressed in AEI publications are those of the authors and do not necessarily reflect the views of the staff, advisory panels, officers, or trustees.

AEI STUDIES ON UNDERSTANDING
ECONOMIC INEQUALITY
Marvin H. Kosters, series editor

THE DISTRIBUTION OF WEALTH: INCREASING INEQUALITY?
John C. Weicher

EARNINGS INEQUALITY: THE INFLUENCE OF CHANGING
OPPORTUNITIES AND CHOICES
Robert H. Haveman

INCOME MOBILITY AND THE MIDDLE CLASS
*Richard V. Burkhauser, Amy D. Crews, Mary C. Daly,
and Stephen P. Jenkins*

INCOME REDISTRIBUTION AND THE REALIGNMENT
OF AMERICAN POLITICS
Nolan M. McCarty, Keith T. Poole, and Howard Rosenthal

RELATIVE WAGE TRENDS, WOMEN'S WORK,
AND FAMILY INCOME
Chinhui Juhn

THE THIRD INDUSTRIAL REVOLUTION: TECHNOLOGY,
PRODUCTIVITY, AND INCOME INEQUALITY
Jeremy Greenwood

WAGE INEQUALITY: INTERNATIONAL COMPARISONS
OF ITS SOURCES
Francine D. Blau and Lawrence M. Kahn